Let's go to Costa Rica!

Costa Rica is a beautiful country located in Central America with a lush and tropical environment, which makes it a widely favored international travel destination. It has a population of 5 million and this tiny country (roughly the size of Lake Michigan), has 5% of the biodiversity in the entire world. It is an adventure paradise and the place to visit for beaches, volcanoes, rainforests and diverse wildlife!

This is our *Costa Rica Family Travel Planner* detailing fun-filled family activities in three destinations including Arenal Volcano (La Fortuna), Monteverde Cloud forest, and one of the most popular beach towns, Tamarindo. A one and two-week travel itinerary is provided to show you how you can plan your trip. There are lots of activities listed if you plan to stay longer than two weeks!

This guide will also help you be well prepared for your trip providing you with information on a few ways to save money, avoid common mistakes, and things to consider about where to stay and how to get around. There is a "What to know before you go" section, Travel Tips and information on What Not to do in Costa Rica. Also included is a list of popular Costa Rican dishes, Must have apps, and some common Terms and Phrases you should know.

If you love the perfect balance of adventures and a relaxing beach holiday, this travel planner is for you!

There is a free travel itinerary template on our website you can download as a planning tool. Find it at:
www.adventurecampitelli.com/shop.

The itinerary is based on flying into and out of Liberia International Airport (LIR). It is possible to fly out of San Jose International Airport (SJO), simply change up the route.

ABOUT US

We are a family of 4 travel enthusiasts & adventurers who left our jobs and schools behind in 2018 to travel the world. Documenting our experiences on YouTube and our website, we are inspired to share our knowledge with you in our family travel guides. We receive many questions from travelers looking for advice and insights about the countries we visit, so we created travel guides to make travel planning much easier.

Unlike daunting, long-winded travel books, our guides are simple, short, easy to read, and written with the family in mind. They're for busy people who don't have the time to sift through multiple websites or pages and pages of information to plan their trip. The guides easily fit into a travel bag, purse or glove compartment and are loaded with lots of fun family activities and itineraries.

LET'S CONNECT!

Email: ContactUs
@adventurecampitelli.com
www.adventurecampitelli.com

CONTENTS

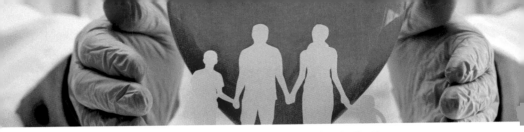

WHAT TO KNOW BEFORE YOU GO

KNOW...

The current rules for entering Costa Rica & the re-entry rules for your own country.

For Canadian and US citizens you require a valid passport and a return ticket to exit Costa Rica within 90 days. You do not require an entry visa. If you are not from the US or Canada find the information at this website: **http://www.costarica-embassy.org/index.php? q=node/72**

KNOW...

What vaccinations are required and recommended.

Rules are always changing so it's a good idea to double check before you leave for your trip. There are certain vaccinations that are recommended when traveling to Costa Rica including:

- Hepatitis A & B
- Typhoid
- Up to date on Measles, Mumps, Rubella (MMR)
- Tetanus
- Flu shot
- Covid-19

Be sure to check with your doctor or local travel clinic.

KNOW...

Where the local hospitals and health clinics are for each area that you stay in. The emergency number in Costa Rica is 911.

La Fortuna (Fortuna Clinic):
This clinic is located on Calle 3 and is for minor health concerns only. Some doctors speak English. Phone: 2479-9501 or 2479-9142. The nearest hospital for major injuries is about an hour away in Ciudad Quesada.

Monteverde (Santa Elana):
For minor health concerns, visitors can call the local Red Cross (Santa Elena; 2645-6128), or be treated at one of several small medical clinics (Consultorio Medico Emergencias Monteverde in Cerro Plano; 2645-7778).

amarindo

rivate Medical Clinic: Pacific Emergencies. Doctors usually charge $60 er walk-in visit, but bilingual emergency medical technicians are on call -hours a day. (2653-2001, Emergencies 8378-8265).

ublic Medical Clinic: EBAIS, a 15-minute drive from town in Villareal.The linic offers free or low-cost walk-in visits (check with your insurance ompany) and 24-hour ambulance and emergency services (2653-0736).

he closest hospitals are in Liberia, about an hour's drive from amarindo.

> NOTE: Unless it is an emergency, check your insurance policy to understand the rules for accessing care.

NOW...

What travel insurance is required including health insurance.

et your insurance company know what activities you will be articipating in to see if extra travel insurance is required. While some ravel insurance may be covered through your credit card or ompany plan, it is very likely that it will not cover some of the ctivities that you plan on doing. For example, hiking, ziplining, ayaking and other activities usually need to be insured separately. lan for the activities you might be doing and insure your family for hese. You can always add activities later.The costs are fairly minimal. on't forget to include trip cancelation and trip interruption insurance s well.

Ve use World Nomads Insurance as they have great coverage and nsure many countries. Visit their website: **ttps://www.worldnomads.com/**. Note that only cover travelers up to ge 70 (age 65 in some areas). Try Insure My Trip if you are over the ge of 70. Website: **https://www.insuremytrip.com/**

efore purchasing insurance check what you are covered for with xisting insurance you have through your job and credit card so you on't purchase more insurance than you need. We found out we were overed by our credit card for trip cancellation.

KNOW...

There is a departure fee when leaving the country.

The cost is $29/person for the departure tax. Most airlines will not include this charge on your tickets. However, double check to be sur[e] The Costa Rica airport departure tax is payable at a special counter at the airport. It can be paid in US dollars or colones. You can also pay by Credit card but they will charge you extra fees. Some hotels will handle this for you, usually for a fee.

KNOW...

The roads are really bad in some areas.

Some of the main roads have had improvements and paving but many are still in poor condition. If you're renting a car, we recommen[d] an SUV (even a small one) to get around, especially if you're heading to hiking trails, waterfalls, etc. For navigating, make sure you use the WAZE app as Apple and Google Maps do not work properly and ma[y] take you to the wrong destination. This happened to us!

KNOW...

The water is safe to drink...mostly.

Surprisingly, I've read that it has some of the safest in the world. Whe[n] we were there we did not have any issues with drinking the tap wate[r] However, exercise caution in the more remote areas and where wate[r] is coming from a tank or water well. If you are concerned, consider these two things:

- *Bring a water purifier or filter or water purification tablets.*
- *Bring activated charcoal which helps with tummy troubles. We always bring these when we travel.*

KNOW...

Costa Rica is expensive!

You might think that Costa Rica is cheap because it is in Central America but this is not true. Hotels, AirBNB's, car rentals, gas prices, and tours are very expensive. Costa Rica is rated as one of the most expensive places to live in Latin America. It is an amazing country bu[t] you pay North American prices. Save money by shopping for grocer[ies] at Walmart & cooking your own food, eating at local mom & pop restaurants, and using local transportation if you are staying in one place and don't need a car rental.

Where to stay

There are plenty of types of accommodations in Costa Rica including resorts, hostels, hotels, and Airbnb's. Our family mostly uses Airbnb's when we travel, giving us more space including a kitchen to cook meals.

How to get around

The best option by far is renting a car if it fits your budget. A vehicle makes it easier to get to many activities listed in this guide, especially with kids. There are many decent car rental companies in Costa Rica.

Taxis:

Red taxis are the official taxis and are regulated by the government with set fares. They have meters, a yellow taxi hat on top and a yellow triangle on the door with the taxi license number. We recommend these as there are many "pirate taxis" around that may scam you.

There are also taxi stands outside the San Jose and Liberia Airport The airport taxis at the San Jose airport are orange and are the only ones authorized to operate there.

Shuttles:

Costa Rica has both private and shared shuttle services. The private shuttles can cost more but you have the shuttle to yourself and they don't make any stops. The shared shuttles usually will make multiple stops to pick up other people. They also require a minimum amount of people to run (e.g. 4 people). Shared shuttles are usually booked through hotels and some hotels offer complimentary shuttle service to and from the airport. There are several private shuttle services companies. This one: **https://www.transportationincostarica.com/** has a good rating but it's a good idea to get 2-3 quotes.

Buses:

Buses are the cheaper option but you need to do a lot of research to find the buses and routes that you need. Buses companies are privately owned so they all have their own bus stations, routes, times and costs. Many bus routes to tourist destinations run from San Jose so you can find something. Look at descriptions and reviews of buses as some are better than others (i.e. cleaner and include air conditioning). This link is a good resource for buses and other info:
https://www.visitcostarica.com/en/costa-rica/bus-itinerary

Where to get food

Grocery Stores
The first thing we do when we arrive at our destination is pick up groce
items, especially breakfast items and snacks. Costa Rica has both larg
grocery stores and smaller ones depending on where you are visiting. A
three areas in this guide have a few stores to choose from. You can loo
up on food at Walmart in Liberia or San Jose to save money before
heading to your first destination.

Farmers Markets
Every area also has its own farmers market, known as La Feria. Here yo
can get a good selection of fresh fruits and veggies sold to you directly
from the farmers. There are usually snacks and street food items as we
The prices can be significantly lower than the grocery stores and usual
take place on Fridays or Saturday mornings.

Dining Out:
Costa Rica has all the traditional North American food like burgers,
pizza, chicken wings, etc., and other international cuisines. They also
have American chains such as McDonald's in the larger cities like San
Jose and Liberia. In our opinion, it's fun to get the full experience when
you travel which includes indulging in the local cuisine. Traditional Cos
Rican food will not disappoint!

Local Costa Rican restaurants are called Sodas. These are small, mom-
and-pop restaurants that serve only traditional Costa Rican food. They
are usually much cheaper than other restaurants and they're great to
experience eating out like a local. Find the ones that seem busy and
filled with locals. *La Tipica* in La Fortuna and *Soda y Marisquería
Marcela* in Tamarindo are family run and excellent!

The biggest meal of the day in Costa Rica is lunch. Making lunch your
main meal will save you money!

In restaurants and hotels, 13% Value Added Tax (VAT) and a 10% tip are
added to the bill. If you receive exceptional service, an additional tip is
much appreciated.

ravel Tips

os to help you be more prepared for your trip to Costa Rica.

urrency:

he colon is the official currency in Costa Rica. The exchange rate varies ut as of August 2022, it was $1 USD to 665 colones. Keep these things in ind to get the most value and to avoid unnecessary hassles:

- Exchange your US dollars for colones once you get to Costa Rica as you'll usually get a better rate.

- Use ATMs but go to banks or busy stores as they are less likely to have skimmers that steal your bank card info. Check with your bank in advance what the fees are for foreign currency.

- Don't use the currency exchanges at the major airports as you'll likely get a worse rate than the ATM or even hotels.

- Use both US Cash (in small bills like $20 or less) and colones to give you payment flexibility.

- Taxis, hotels, and restaurant chains will accept US dollars. We found a few places that only accepted US dollars.

- Use colones in smaller markets and roadside stands. They will likely accept US dollars but will not give you the right exchange rate.

- Let your bank know you are leaving the country so your credit card isn't blocked leaving you without access to credit. We suggest not using your main credit card and changing your security pin when you get home.

- As a guide, for our family of four, we brought about $1000 total (US and Colones) for a two-week holiday. We paid for some items like tours on our credit card.

ing Water Shoes

his seems minor but I sure could have used these the last time I visited. your visiting waterfalls or going rafting, they really come in handy

Car Rentals

The usual rental companies are there including Enterprise, Hertz, Budget, Thrifty's, etc. Plus there are a few local Costa Rican companies.

The biggest tip here is to understand the full cost of your car rental. If you book through 3rd party sites like Expedia or Kayak, they only show you the rental price, not all the extra fees (including insurance) and taxes so when you arrive to pick up your rental, you will be shocked at the extra costs. Our recommendation is to go directly to each of the companies' Costa Rica pages and compare prices online directly. Make sure you scroll to see the final costs. We thought our rental was $600 only to find out when we got there that the price was $900 (with the extra insurance).

There are three types of insurance sold by car rental companies.

1) **3rd Party Liability insurance** - it is mandatory and not covered by your credit card or any coverage you have at home. This insurance covers damages to other people, their car, or property. It doesn't cover your rental car. Most foreign insurance companies will not provide third-party insurance in Costa Rica so you must buy it there. It costs an extra $15-$25+ USD per day. This makes a big difference in your price!

2) **Collision Damage or Loss Damage insurance** - this is optional and reduces your liability for your car rental to the deductible amount (Approx $1500-$3000USD) if you get into an accident. The cost ranges from $US 15-40 per day depending on the company and vehicle. You are still responsible for all losses or damages in the case of negligence, vandalism, road damage, or theft.

3) **Zero Liability insurance** - this is optional and considered full coverage insurance. It is intended to reduce your liability to zero when combined with the other two policies. For example, it covers damage done to the car from theft. The cost ranges from $US 5-20 per day in addition to the other insurances depending on the fine print and vehicle.

The above two insurances may be covered by your credit card but find this out before renting so you understand your coverage, otherwise, you will be charged when you pick up your vehicle. You also have to provide proof of car insurance so bring the printed proof of the coverage with you.

> **Expert tip:** Take a video or lots of pictures of the car both inside and out so you're not held responsible for damage you didn't cause.

Cell Phone Plans

You have 3 options: 1) add a travel plan to your regular cell phone plan, 2) purchase a pre-paid physical SIM card. 3) Purchase an eSIM (embedded SIM) card. Option 1 is far more expensive and you will often get a slower connection. You can buy SIM cards at the airport (which cost more), in some supermarkets or at Costa Rica telephone companies. **Kolbi** seems to have the best coverage. You will get a local phone number and data. To purchase a SIM card you will need your passport ID and cash. When you replace your SIM card, make sure you put your SIM card in a safe place and do not lose it! The SIM cards usually come with a holder for your card. The 3rd (newer option) is the eSIM card which you order online, receive a code on your phone, follow the instructions, enter the code, change the settings and connect to a local network in Costa Rica. With an eSIM, you don't need to go to a store, wait for the mail, or fiddle with a tiny chip. You can also often use two different lines on the same device, or switch between different plans depending on where you are.
Here is one company that offers eSIMs: **https://www.airalo.com/costa-rica-esim**

Be sure to wear bug spray

Like many lush tropical places, Costa Rica has a lot of bugs including Mosquitoes which can carry diseases like the Zika virus or Dengue fever. Beyond the health risks, bites can be so itchy and uncomfortable. I recommend bringing insect repellent versus trying to buy it there as it can be more expensive and sometimes hard to find. Wear long pants, and long-sleeved shirts on hikes and try to stay indoors at dawn and dusk when they are most active. If you do get bit, I find "After bite" over-the-counter medication helps relieve some of the itching. I always bring this with me when I travel to a tropical country.

Protect yourself from the Sun!

The sun in Cost Rica is crazy strong and it is very easy to get burnt. Consider these tips:

- Wear sunscreen – I wear at least 30.
- Wear sunglasses with UV protection. UV sun shirts are great for the beach.
- Wear a large brimmed hat.
- Look for shade under a tree or beach umbrella.

What NOT to do in Costa Rica

We love visiting Costa Rica and it's a great place to take kids however, there are a few things NOT to do that you should be aware of.

These Dont's will help make your vacation easier and avoid some mistakes.

This may seem obvious but don't arrive without booking a place or car rental – especially during high season.
- This is a very common mistake. Booking in advance gives you more choices so you can find something within your price range and the features that you are looking for.
- Costa Rica's high season is December through April and the busiest and most expensive times are Christmas, New Years and Easter week.
- Car rentals and hotel rooms book up very fast, so make sure you start looking around at least 2 months before your trip if visiting during those times. We start our planning 4-6 months in advance

Don't plan to go to too many places
When you look at a map, Costa Rica looks small but it takes a long time to get anywhere as many roads are in poor condition, windy and have slow speed limits. Getting from one place to another will take 2 to 4 time longer than you're used to. There are so many activities to do in every area that you don't need to move around too much. In two weeks, we find that 3 destinations are perfect if you like to experience different places.

Don't pick the flowers or plants
You might go for a walk and see beautiful flowers or plant life that is so tempting to take. The reason we mention this is that In Costa Rica, vegetation is strictly protected by the government and it could be the equivalent of a felony if you are caught doing this.

Don't take home any shells from the beach
It is so tempting to take home beautiful sea shells from the beach but like the plant life, it is illegal to take them from the beach and out of the country.

Don't go nude at the beach or wear a bathing suit off the beach

This is typically frowned upon as Costa Rica is a modest country however, I believe there are a few beaches that allow nudity but make sure you find out which ones first!

Don't buy your Souvenirs at the Airport

You will end up paying much more and the prices are non-negotiable. There are many markets and small shops in Costa Rica that you can usually negotiate the price on and it's a much more fun experience. You can usually find more unique items as well.

Don't flush your toilet paper down the toilet

The country's plumbing was never built to accommodate an excessive amount of toilet paper and, since many systems are septic or composting, you'll find 'toilet paper bins' in every toilet stall, all over the country. This took us a bit to get used to but this is not uncommon in other countries as well or homes with septic systems.

Don't leave valuables visible in your car

This is common sense and applies pretty much anywhere but there is particularly high theft in Costa Rica so make sure you keep your valuables with you at all times. I didn't bring any expensive jewelry or even my wedding ring. Some parking lots have attendants that will watch your vehicle and it only costs $.40 - 1USD.

Don't be afraid to try to speak a little Spanish with the locals

They will usually appreciate the effort and we found that most did not speak English. Use google translate or another app or go old school and bring a small dictionary. Even better, learn basic words before your trip.

What NOT to do - Wildlife

Costa Rica has many amazing animals but there are some things you shouldn't do when it comes to the wildlife. Many of these seem obvious but they actually happen. Don't let the information covered here discourage you from going to this spectacular country. It is intended to give you a few tips to be more comfortable and prepared.

Don't swim in Rivers or murky water

There are crocodiles in some of the rivers in Costa Rica and even some sharks have swlm up stream from the ocean into rivers.

Don't feed the monkeys or any wildlife

In Costa Rica, there are lots of cute monkeys and they are used to tourists feeding them, but feeding them is not only illegal, but also harmful to them and you. Our food isn't monkey food so they shouldn't be eating it. They may get lazy and not find their own food, or they may become aggressive and steal your food or other belongings.

Don't go near the tiny cute frogs

There are tiny colourful frogs called poison dart frogs and they are one of the most poisonous frogs on the planet. They live in the rainforests. They are only about 2-3 centimetres and have enough venom to kill ten grown men if the venom gets into the bloodstream. They stay away from people, just don't try to catch or touch them if you see them.

Don't forget to shake out your shoes before putting them on and don't leave your suitcases and bags open.

Spiders and scorpion's like to hide in dark places and may sneak into your shoes when you are not wearing them. You wouldn't want to get a bite or sting from these creatures so as a precaution, just shake out you shoes before you put them on. Also, keep your luggage and bags zipped tight.

Don't get close to the Ants

They have lots of different types of ants there like fire ants, leaf-cutter ants, army ants and bullet ants which won't kill you but can have a real painful sting. We saw a bunch of different types of ants on a night nature walk we did. It's fun to watch them but keep your distance.

Don't go off marked trails when hiking and watch for snakes

Many snakes live in Costa Rica including venomous snakes, so it's important to be aware if you are going on any hikes. They are scared of people, typically stay away and are most active at night. Bites are rare but it isn't a good idea to veer off marked trails. People do occasionally get bit and there is a treatment for bites if this happens.

Costa Rican dishes

Costa Rican cuisine is fairly mild (not a lot of spice), with rice and beans being the staple of most of the meals, often served three times a day. The meals are well-balanced, made up of a lot of fruits and vegetables, and cooked from scratch using fresh ingredients. Here are a few we loved:

Gallo Pinto
Classic Costa Rican breakfast made up of rice & beans mixed together, served with sour cream and avocado. Cilantro, onions and salsa are included for added falvor.

Casado
The most traditional dish. Consists of rice, beans, salad, tortillas and choice of pork, chicken, beef or fish. It usually comes with fresh fruit juice.

Tamale
 filling of chicken, beef or pork and ground cornmeal wrapped in plantain leaves. Less spicy than its Mexican counterpart.

Sopa Negra
A soup made of black beans, cilantro, onion and egg. Very filling!

Arroz con Leche
The Costa Rican version of rice pudding. White rice cooked in milk, sugar, lemon zest, raisins and cinnamon.

Pipa Fria
s cold coconut water and is available all over Costa Rica. It can be found rom roadside vendors to people selling it at the beach. We loved this refreshing drink!

Common terms and phrases

When going to Costa Rica it's handy to know some of the common phrases and words that will make your trip a little easier.

Pura Vida - life is good!
It means "Pure Life" and is used in many different ways like nice to meet you, see you later, you're welcome. It represents a laid-back way of life that is good or how someone is feeling.

Tico - a Costa Rican Man
This word is short for Costa Rican man and Tica is for a woman. For a group of Costa Rican people, usually, Ticos is used.

Mae - dude
Used among friends, it means guy, dude or bro.

A cachete - good
Describes something is really good or doing good.

Tuanis - cool
Means cool, awesome.

Dónde está el baño?
Where is the bathroom?

Cuánto cuesta?
How much does it cost?

No hablo español.
I don't speak Spanish.

Habla inglés?
Do you speak English?

Two Week Sample Itinerary

This sample itinerary is an idea of how you can plan your two week vacation. There are even more activities included in this guide to make that perfect itinerary for your family.

- **Day 1:** Arrive at Liberia International Airport (LIR) and head to La Fortuna, a small town just outside Arenal National Park.
  - Approximately 3 hours by car.

- **Days 2-5:** Arenal and La Fortuna
  - Day 2 - Visit La Fortuna Waterfall/Hike 1968 Park
  - Day 3 - Mistico Hanging Bridges/Coffee & Chocolate Tour
  - Day 4 - Horse Back Riding/Sloth Watching Tour
  - Day 5 - Tabacon Hot Springs

- **Days 6-8**: Monteverde Cloud Forest
  - Day 6 - Drive to Monteverde (approx. 3.5 hours by car). Get settled and get groceries.
  - Day 7 - Hike Monteverde Cloud Forest Preserve/Hummingbird Garden.
  - Day 8 - Ziplining/Night Walk Tour.

- **Days 9-12:** Tamarindo beach town.
  - Day 9 - Drive to Tamarindo (approximtely 3 hours by car). Go to Tamarindo beach.
  - Day 10 - Mangrove Estuary Boat Tour/Playa Flamingo beach.
  - Day 11 - Catamaran Tour/Playa Avellanas Beach
  - Day 12 - Langosta Beach Club

- **Days 13-14**: Drive back to Liberia and relax at a hotel near the airport. Visit Ponderosa Adventure Park. Depart home.

One Week Sample Itinerary

If you only have 7 days in Costa Rica, below is an example itinerary you can follow.

- **Day 1:** Arrive at Liberia International Airport (LIR) and head to La Fortuna, a small town just outside Arenal National Park.
  - Approximately 3 hours by car.

- **Days 2-3:** Arenal and La Fortuna
  - Day 2 - Visit La Fortuna Waterfall/Hike 1968 Park
  - Day 3 - Mistico Hanging Bridges/Tabacon Hot Springs

- **Days 4-5:** Tamarindo beach town.
  - Day 4 - Drive to Tamarindo (approximtely 3 hours by car). G to Tamarindo beach.
  - Day 5 - Mangrove Estuary Boat Tour/Playa Langosta Beach Club or Flamingo Beach.

- **Days 6-7**: Drive back to Liberia to depart home.
  - Day 6 - Mangrove Estuary Boat Tour/Drive to Liberia.
  - Day 7 - Depart Home.

Alternatively, spend your week in Tamarindo as there are so many activities to do there!

Must Have Apps

These helpful apps will help make your vacation in Costa Rica smoother.

Download Before You Leave

Waze
This works the best for navigation! Google Maps does not work well.

Trip Advisor
Good for getting reviews of any activities you want to do.

Uber
This ride-hailing app is in bigger population areas like San Jose.

OIJ CRSafe
App to help keep tourists safe including emergency numbers

MyCurrency
Use this to compare currency exhange rates.

Google Translate
You'll need to use a little bit of Spanish as not everyone speaks English.

WhatsApp
The best way to communicate in Costa Rica.

CRMaps
Lists attractions, lodging, restaurants, transportation and tourist spots. Very helpful!

ARENAL VOLCANO NATIONAL PARK

Located in northern Costa Rica, Arenal Volcano National Park, known as the adventure capital, is one of the most popular destinations in Costa Rica. The Arenal Volcano is the most recognizable Volcano in Costa Rica, and was one of the most active volcanoes in the world until 2010. With so much to offer, the area also boasts a lush rainforest, spectacular waterfalls and Costa Rica's biggest lake, lake Arenal. There are an endless amount of fun activities to do with your family!

To keep everyone's energy level high and strike a balance of activity and relaxation time, our family mostly planned one activity per day. However, if you are looking to do more than this, a list of other options is provided.

La Fortuna is Arenal's main town and has hotels, shopping, supermarkets, pharmacies, banks, shops, restaurants and tours. It is located just 17.7km (11 miles) east of the Arenal volcano.

ARENAL VOLCANO NATIONAL PARK

La Fortuna waterfall

- La Fortuna waterfall is a powerful 70 meter high waterfall in the jungle fed by the Tenorio River. It plummets into an emerald green pool below where you can go for a refreshing swim. People come from all over the world to see this waterfall.

- The waterfall is located just a few Km/Mi outside of the town of La Fortuna at the base of the Cerro Chato volcano. It is located in a biological reserve of 210 acres of tropical wet forest and is part of Arenal Volcano National Park.

- There is no public bus or shuttle service to get there so you will need to drive or take a taxi.

- The cost is $18 USD per adult and $5 USD for kids. The hours are 7am to 5pm every day.

- This is one of the most visited waterfalls in Costa Rica so get there early to avoid big crowds.

- There are change rooms, a restaurant and souvenir shop at the trail head as well as a nice viewing platform to take photos before you head down.

- It takes about 15 minutes to hike down a path of a few hundred stairs to the waterfall. Some of the stairs are quite steep but there are handrails and benches along the way. You can't bring strollers on the path.

- Plan 3-4 hours here. No guide necessary.

Expert Tip: Wear good shoes or hiking sandals for the walk. Bring water shoes and a bathing suit to go for a dip!

Mistico Park hanging bridges

- This is a beautiful nature reserve park that is located 20 KM (12.5 miles) west of La Fortuna. You can either drive or some hotels offer transportation. There are no public buses that go there. It takes about 30 minutes to get there from La Fortuna.

- You are required to purchase your tickets online in advance. Book your tickets:
  https://www.misticopark.com

- The unguided tour costs $26 USD per adult and free for kids under the age of 10. You can also do a guided tour for $40 USD per adult and $14 USD per child. Guides are knowledgeable and know how to spot the animals that can be difficult to see.

- The park is open from 6am to 4:30pm and the latest time they will let you in is 3:50pm.

- The trail is roughly 2.5km long and will take about 2-3 hours to do as you will likely stop to admire all the animals and beautiful vegetation.

- There is a well marked path that takes you through the lush thick vegetation rain forest and over 16 hanging bridges suspended overtop of gorges and tree canopies.

- Some of the bridges are quite high up (up to 55 metres (147 feet)) and may bother you if you have a fear of heights. They are completely safe and closed in on the sides. It's a good opportunity to conquer that fear!

- There is so much beautiful nature here and you may be able to see different types of birds, monkeys, sloths, snakes and frogs as well as a spectacular view of Arenal Volcano

Expert Tip: Wear closed toe shoes, insect repellent and don forget to bring lots of water and your camera!

Coffee and chocolate tasting tour

- Both Cocoa and coffee beans are grown in Costa Rica and it's worth going on a tour to learn about their biggest exports. Costa Rica's coffee beans have won competitions across the world!

- You learn about the entire process including seeing the plants in the field, to harvesting, to roasting (for coffee), to grinding (for chocolate) and the best part of all, tasting!

- The cost is around $40 USD per adult, $30 USD for students. and kids 9 and under are Free. It takes about 2-3 hours and kids love tasting the chocolate!

- There are a couple of highly rated tours including Don Juan Tours La Fortuna: **(https://www.donjuantours.com/)** and North Fields Coffee and Chocolate Tour: **(https://northfieldscafe.business.site/)**.

Hike Arenal 1968 Park

- This park got its name from the Arenal Volcano eruption of 1968, a huge eruption that destroyed 3 towns, ruined crops, killed several people and created huge lava fields down the volcano.

- The big draw of these trails is you get close views of Arenal Volcano, old lava flows and a view of Lake Arenal. It is a beautiful trail to hike with well marked with pathways.

- It is located 16 KM (10 miles) west of La Fortuna on route 142, then left onto Calle Real El Castil that goes to Arenal Volcano National Park. Drive, take a taxi or arrange a tour with transportation as there are no public buses that go there. It takes about 20-25 minutes to get there from La Fortuna. There is a visitor centre and parking area.

- The cost is $17 USD per adult and kids under 1. are free. The hours for this park are 8am-6pm daily.

- There are two trails. The red trail, called the Lava Flow 1968 trail, is 2.5 km (1.55 mi) and take about an hour. The yellow trail, called the Forest trail is 4.5km (2.8 mi) trail takes about 2. hours and it includes both trails. The yellow trail is rated as more difficult with lots of loos gravel and rocks. We did this trail with our kic who were ages 7 and 11 at the time without issue, however they are used to hiking

- Both trails take you through the forest, acros lava fields and to the same spot with spectacular views of the Volcano and Areno lake.

- At the end, treat yourself to a tropical drink and a snack at the cafeteria.

> **Expert Tip:** Wear good shoes for hiking, don't forget to bring lots of water and your rain jacket.

Relax at Tabacon Falls Resort & Spa

- Tabacon Thermal Resort & Spa is a 5 star resort located at the base of Arenal Volcano near La Fortuna. In addition to the natural thermal hot springs, there are spa services, overnight accommodations and a really nice restaurant.

- With its stunning cascading falls surrounded by lush tropical rainforest, it is by far, the best hot springs we have ever been to!

- A natural volcanic river called Rio Chollin, heated by Arenal Volcano flows through the resort to make the mineralized hot springs. Thousands of gallons of water are naturally flowing every minute. These springs cascade down the volcano to form waterfalls, streams and little pools that you sit in, all surrounded by lush tropical gardens. The perfect backdrop of stunning beauty and relaxation!

- The rocks are black and the water looks cool however, they are very warm and the further up you climb, the hotter they are. The river-pool temperatures range from 72 to 105 degrees Fahrenheit.

- You can choose to stay overnight at the resort, do a full day pass or a morning pass.

- The full day experience includes lunch & dinner and costs $105 USD per adult and $40 USD per child.

- The 4 hours experience (morning or afternoon) is $85 USD per adult and $38 USD per child and includes either lunch or dinner depending on the time of day that you go. We found the 4 hours experience to be enough time.

- There are a couple of other options as well including early morning and night pass.

- The hours are 10am to 10pm.

- If you stay at the resort you have free access to the mineral springs.

- There is a man made pool in the resort (heated by the springs) with a swim up bar and waterside which is an added bonus if you have kids.

- Visit: **https://www.tabacon.com/**

- There are other hotels with hot springs that are less expensive, however they are just heated man-made pools from the hot springs

Expert Tip: Reserve in advance as it might book up!

FREE EXPERIENCE:
if you want a free experience of the mineral springs, you can park at the side of the road (locals will ask for a small "fee" to park) and walk downhill (to the right of the resort) to the river where you will be at a bottom of a bridge. You can go right or left to find a good spot. Lie down and enjoy the experience of the thermal water. This is nothing like you'll ever experience! In our opinion, if you can splurge for the resort experience, it's definitely worth the once in a lifetime experience!

Other Things to do In Arenal

If you want to pack more activities into your time in Arenal, these adventure activities are highly rated and worth looking into.

Sky Trek Ziplines

Costa Rica is known for ziplining and Arenal is an amazing place to do it. The cost is $84 USD for adults and $58 USD for kids.

Sky Walk Hanging Bridges

This is a beautiful guided 4km (2.5 mi) tour on a suspension bridge and trails overlooking the treetops. The cost is $41 USD for adults and $28 USD for kids.

Sky Tram

A Gondola takes you up over the mountain for amazing views of the rain forest, volcano and lake. A fun lowkey activity. The cost is $48 USD for adults and $33 USD for kids.

Sky Wild Kayaking

A guided kayak tour on beautiful Lake Arenal. The cost is $49 USD for adults and $34 USD for kids.

Sky Wild Bikes

A guided mountain bike around Lake Arenal. The cost is $49 USD for adults and $34 USD for kids. Activities can be combined in packages. See their website at **https://skyadventures.travel/**

Horseback Riding

There are several companies offering horseback rides to explore the Costa Rican rainforest. Rides are usually 2-3 hours in length and prices range from about $60-$75 USD per person.

Sloth Watching Tour

This is a fun activity for the family. It is located in the heart of La Fortuna and is a 2km long guided walking tour where you get to see sloths in their natural habitat. The tour takes one and a half hours. The cost is $97 for adults and $47 for kids. They also offer other tours such as bird watching, night walks, coffee, chocolate and sugar cane tours. Find out more information on their website: **https://www.slothwatchingtrail.com/**

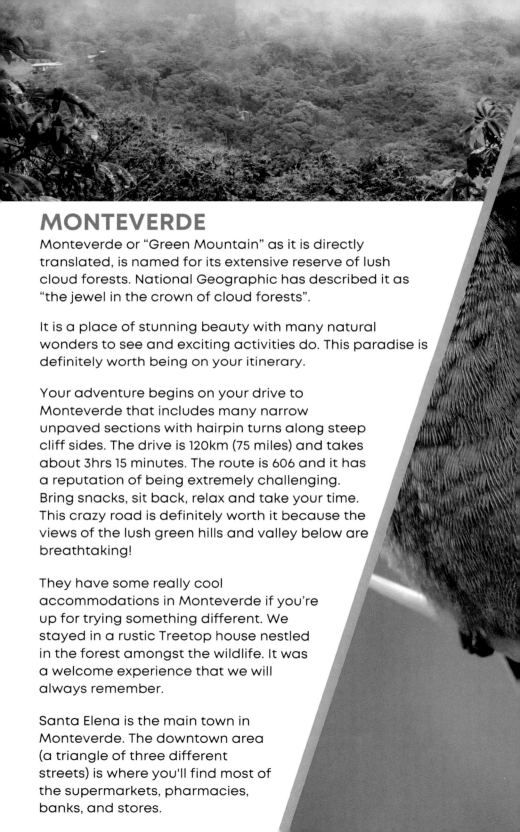

MONTEVERDE

Monteverde or "Green Mountain" as it is directly translated, is named for its extensive reserve of lush cloud forests. National Geographic has described it as "the jewel in the crown of cloud forests".

It is a place of stunning beauty with many natural wonders to see and exciting activities do. This paradise is definitely worth being on your itinerary.

Your adventure begins on your drive to Monteverde that includes many narrow unpaved sections with hairpin turns along steep cliff sides. The drive is 120km (75 miles) and takes about 3hrs 15 minutes. The route is 606 and it has a reputation of being extremely challenging. Bring snacks, sit back, relax and take your time. This crazy road is definitely worth it because the views of the lush green hills and valley below are breathtaking!

They have some really cool accommodations in Monteverde if you're up for trying something different. We stayed in a rustic Treetop house nestled in the forest amongst the wildlife. It was a welcome experience that we will always remember.

Santa Elena is the main town in Monteverde. The downtown area (a triangle of three different streets) is where you'll find most of the supermarkets, pharmacies, banks, and stores.

Get to know Monteverde and Santa Elena

- Check in, pick up some food, take a little walk around and get familiar with the area. We recommend you go for dinner in Santa Elena.

- There is a great selection of restaurants featuring international and local cuisine, bars, and cute little shops that make it a great place to explore.

Night Walk Tour

- This is definitely a must! It's very informative and fun to learn about all the creatures that are out at night. We saw lots of animals and insects including various types of sleeping birds, a tarantula, scorpion and coati (raccoon type species). Other animals you may see include snakes, armadillos, sloths and much more.

- There are a few private reserves that offer night walks including Santamaria Night Walk, http://nightwalkssantamarias.com, https://kinkajounightwalk.com and https://ficustrails.com which all have decent ratings.

- Most walks start sometime between 6pm and 8:30 pm and last for about 2 hours.

- The cost is in the range of $25-$30 USD and includes transportation from your accommodations.

Expert Tip: Wear good shoes for hiking, wear bug spray and your rain jacket!

Hike through Monteverde Cloud Forest Reserve

- The Monteverde Cloud Forest Reserve was created in 1972 to protect the endangered cloud forest habitat from logging. People come to this region to observe the exotic highland bird species and the cloud forest canopy. This reserve has over 25,000 acres of land that protects river, rainforest, and cloud forest habitats.

- There are over 100 species of animals including monkeys, porcupines, deer, sloths, jaguars, and pumas. There are many species of reptiles and amphibians including lizards, snakes, and numerous types of frogs.

- Monteverde is also known for exotic birds including emerald toucannettes, toucans, and many species of hummingbirds.

- The reserve is open from 7 AM – 4 PM daily and there are public bathrooms and a cafeteria at the entrance. The entrance fee is $25 USD per adult and $12 USD per child under 12. You can do self-guided or hire a guide for approximately $20 USD extra.

- A guide will not take you through all the trails but will provide you with a lot of information and are trained to spot wildlife you may not see. If you want to explore all the trails, it is probably best to hike them on your own.

- There are 6 main trails to explore beneath the forest canopy. Some trails are short and only take about 10 minutes to complete and the longer trails are about 1-2 km (0.6-1.2 miles) and wind around swamps and waterfalls. The trails are well signed and well maintained.

- The Sendero Nubloso trail (1125 meters) brings you to viewpoint where you can stand on the continental divide and see the Pacific and Caribbean oceans. (A continental divide is a natural boundary that separates a continent's river systems that feed into different bodies of water or oceans).

- The hike will take about 3-4 hours giving you enough time to take photos.

Directions

- It is an approximately 8-minute drive on Route 620 driving Southeast of Santa Elena. There is a parking lot there with a huge sign. A shuttle will take you to the entrance of the reserve. It costs $5 US roundtrip for the shuttle and parking.

- There is a shuttle that costs $5 USD one way from downtown Santa Elena which takes you to the Monte Verde Cloud Forest Reserve. The number for the shuttle service is 2645-6332.

- There is a public bus that goes there from downtown Santa Elena and the cost is $1 USD each way.

- Taxi is another option which costs approximately $10 USD. Taxis in Monteverde are not metered so it's best to negotiate before you get in. A pricing guide should be available in the taxi.

Expert Tip: Wear good shoes, long pants and long sleeves as it can get cool. Bring lots of water and your in jacket!

Go Ziplining through the Cloud Forest.

- Costa Rica is one of the best places to go ziplining! Imagine careening overtop a rainforest canopy in the most beautiful setting. This is an experience you've got to try at least once in your life.

- Most areas in Costa Rica have zipline tours and we chose to do ours in Monteverde. There are a few companies that offer zipline tours including: Selvatura Adventure Park (https://selvatura.com), Sky Adventures (https://skyadventures.travel/monteverde/) and The Original Canopy Tour (https://originalcanopy.com/). All of these companies received very good ratings. We went with Selvatura.

- Zipline tours takes approximately 2.5 hours but longer if you add other activities.

- The cost varies depending on the company. At Selvatura, the cost is $55 USD per adult and $28 USD for kids under 12.

- Selvatura Adventure Park is a 20 minute drive (6.5km) or 4mi Northeast from Santa Elena. It is open everyday from 7am to 4pm and you should reserve in advance.

- Most zipline companies include transportation from main hotels in Monteverde but not from AirBnb's, so you will need to arrange your own transportation if you are not staying at a hotel.

- Wear long pants or long shorts for the best comfort. You get a small locker to store your walle phone and keys.

- It's a thrilling experience reaching heights of abou 100m (328 ft) and speeds as high as 70km (44mi) pe hour on some ziplines. Before the last cable, there' a tarzan swing where you jump off a tall platform and swing taking you to the ground. Don't worry you're harnessed in!

- The last cable you also have the option of going full Superman or going as a double. The Superman costs $11 USD extra. We opted for doubling up but the Superman looks awesome!

- A good way to get over your fear of heights and it totally doable for most people and most ages.

- Kids younger than age 4 (5 on some ziplines) are usually not able to participate and kids ages 4-9 typically need to ride tandem with an adult. Our daughter was 7 at the time and went by herself without issue.

- Most zipline tours can be paired with other activities which saves you a bit of $ when combined as a package.

Expert Tip: You will want to wear closed toed shoes to protect you feet!

Other Things to do In Monteverde

If you want to pack more activities into your time in Monteverde or swap out activities listed above, check these out!

Selvatura Park (https://selvatura.com) has activities you can pair with their ziplines including:

Hanging Bridges

The treetop walkway is a fun way to experience the cloud forest from up as high as birds fly, around 170ft up on a 2.5km (1.9mi) trail on various suspension bridges. The cost is $39 USD for adults and $28 USD for kids.

Butterfly Garden

Take a guided tour of a cool dome-shaped structure to see more than 30 species of butterflies. The cost is $17 USD for adults and kids.

Hummingbird Garden

Take a guided tour of a cool dome-shaped structure to see more than 30 species of butterflies. The cost is $17 USD for adults and kids.

Coffee & Chocolate Tour

If you didn't do a chocolate tour in Arenal, then you might want to do one here. Two companies to check out our Don Juan Tours Monteverde or Cabure Tours: ·(https://donjuantours.com/monteverde-chocolate-coffee-tours) or Cabure Tours (http://cabure.net/Tours/Tours.html).

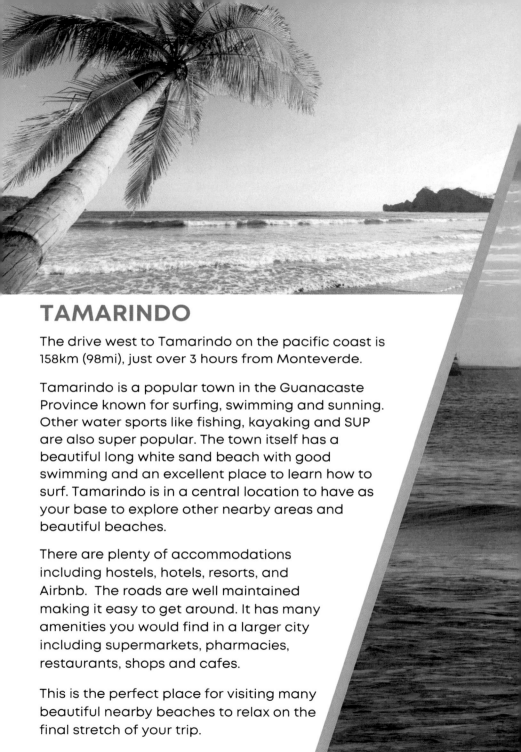

TAMARINDO

The drive west to Tamarindo on the pacific coast is 158km (98mi), just over 3 hours from Monteverde.

Tamarindo is a popular town in the Guanacaste Province known for surfing, swimming and sunning. Other water sports like fishing, kayaking and SUP are also super popular. The town itself has a beautiful long white sand beach with good swimming and an excellent place to learn how to surf. Tamarindo is in a central location to have as your base to explore other nearby areas and beautiful beaches.

There are plenty of accommodations including hostels, hotels, resorts, and Airbnb. The roads are well maintained making it easy to get around. It has many amenities you would find in a larger city including supermarkets, pharmacies, restaurants, shops and cafes.

This is the perfect place for visiting many beautiful nearby beaches to relax on the final stretch of your trip.

This place is super busy during Spring Break with packed beaches and slow-moving traffic.

Tamarindo Beach

- Check in, unpack and explore the town and Tamarindo beach. Don't forget to pick up some groceries at a nearby market. There a few to choose from in Tamarindo. Kids always need lots of snacks!

- Tamarindo beach is 3.5km long (2mi) along the main road. It's great for swimming, relaxing and learning how to surf.

- For dinner, there are many places to choose from including cafes, restaurants, food trucks/street food vendors all over Tamarindo. We recommend trying a Soda for some authentic local cuisine!

Take in the Sunset!

- Costa Rica is known for its beautiful sunsets and Tamarindo beach is one of the best places to catch an amazing sunset. The sun sets early here so make sure you head down to the beach by about 5pm as the sun starts to go down before 5:30pm.

Take a Mangrove Estuary Boat Tour.

- Located between Tamarindo Beach and Play Grande, a calm estuary and mangrove forest exists inside the Tamarindo National Wildlife Refuge which forms part of Las Baulas National Park. This estuary (an area where the Tamarindo freshwater River meets the ocean) is teeming with Wildlife.

- A few companies offer boat tours and they are about 3 hours.

- Wildlife sightings can include iguanas, crocodiles, turtles and lots of different types of birds such as different species of herons, hocks and eagles.

- Las Balulas National Park is known as being one of the nesting sites of Leatherback and Pacific green turtles.

- During the boat tour you will get off the boat into the national park to spot howler monkeys raccoons and other wildlife native to this area

- Most of the tour companies offer transportation if you're staying in the Tamarindo area plus water and a snack.

- The cost is about $35-45 USD per adult and $2! USD per child. You can usually choose between a few times during the day.

- Most tours have good ratings. Here's a link to one of them (**https://www.nativeswaycostarica.com/tour item/tamarindo-estuary-boat-tour/**)

Expert Tip: Wear insect repellent, sunscreen, and a hat.

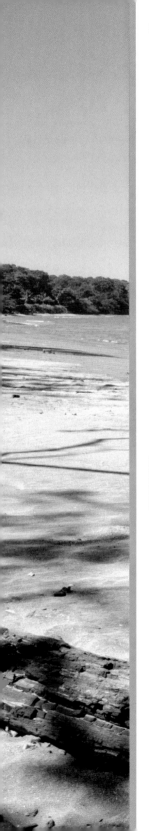

Playa Flamingo beach

- Flamingo is a small high end beach town that has luxury condos, mansions and luxury hotels.

- Play Flamingo is considered one of the most beautiful beaches in Costa Rica. This tropical beach paradise has crystal blue waters and white sand. When you picture a beach, this is usually what comes to mind. There are a lot of fun activities you can do here such as scuba diving, surfing, and body boarding. This crescent shaped beach was one of our favorites!

- Playa Flamingo beach is 22km (14mi) north of Tamarindo and takes approximately 30 minutes to get there.

- You can drive, take a taxi, a shuttle or even the local bus which you can catch along the main street in Tamarindo that only costs about $1 USD each way. These public buses go to many popular beaches near Tamarindo.

Expert Tip: Bring a beach umbrella as the sun can get quite intense.

Playa Avellanas Beach

- Playa Avellanas, or little Hawaii as it's referred to by the locals, is a great surfing beach with waves that can reach up to 5 meters (16 ft) at the North end of the beach.

- This tranquil secluded white sand beach is much less busy than Tamarindo beach.

- It is also known for its cool beachside restaurant called Lola's, named after a 400kg pig named Lola who used to greet you while you dined and could also be seen playing in the waves at the beach.

- Lola has passed away but there are a couple of other pigs there now which is fun for the kids.

- The beach has a cool backdrop of mangroves and trees so it's fairly easy to find a spot in the shade.

- To get there, drive south from Tamarindo about 18km (11mi), about 30 minutes. The best way to get there is to drive, take a shuttle, or a taxi.

- There is a small parking lot at the entrance to the beach. There are usually parking guards there that show you where to park and watch out for your car. In return, you give them a small tip like 1000 colones or less.

Expert Tip: Bring lots of water and snacks if you don't plan to dine at Lola's as there isn't anything close by.

Go on a Catamaran Tour

- This was one of the highlights of our vacation in Costa Rica.

- A Catamaran tour will cost around $75-$95 USD per adult and $65 USD per child for about a 4 hour tour. We went with Marlin del Rey **(https://marlindelrey.com)**. Morning tours are slightly less expensive.

- The tour includes sailing out to a remote location to snorkel and kayak in the beautiful clear ocean waters. The tour includes lunch that is served in a calm secluded bay offering traditional Costa Rican food, fresh fruit, and drinks.

- Make sure to keep your eye out for marine wildlife such as dolphins, sea turtles and whales.

> **Expert Tip:** We like to bring our own snorkel and mask. Don't forget reef safe sunscreen!

Shopping in Tamarindo

- If you love to shop at the local markets and checking artisan wares, Tamarindo has you covered. There is a wide selection of crafts and souvenirs, plenty of them hand made by locals. Plus lots of clothing shops in which you can find nice beach wear.

Playa Langosta

- Playa Langosta is a town that is much smaller and less busy than Tamarindo.

- Located just 2km (1mi) south of Tamarindo, the beach is known as one of the more luxurious beaches with beautiful white sand, amazing surfing waves and a stunning shoreline.

- We highly recommend you visit **Langosta Beach Club,** a private club that has day pass access for visitors. It has a gorgeous outdoor pool with loungers and cabanas, a fitness club, restaurant, and bar.

- The cost of a day pass is $30USD and children under 18 are Free with an adult.

- Reserve in advance, get there early and enjoy an amazing day there!

Other Things to do In Tamarindo

Visit more beautiful beaches near Tamarindo!

Playa Grande Beach

Playa Grande beach (located North of Tamarindo) is miles long of fine pale sand, perfect to long strolls on the beach. This beach is in a protected national park of Las Baulas. Leatherback turtles, the larges sea turtle, come to nest between October and May.

Playa Conchal

Playa Conchal is a beautiful beach that is made up of millions of crushed shells giving it a pinkish hue. The beach gets its name from the Spanish word for shell, "concha". The beautiful clear, warm water is great for swimming or snorkeling. There are many tropical fish in the area and sometimes sting rays frequent the area. There are plenty of water activities there such as jet skiing, kayaking and Standup Paddle board.

Other Awesome Activities

Surfing Lessons

Tamarindo beach is a popular destination for surfing because of its beautiful beaches, long waves and awesome weather. It is also a good spot to learn how to surf as the waves aren't too high. Lessons are offered for all age groups and cost approximately $50.00 USD for 2 hours including Surf Board.

ATV Tours

A fun tour that takes you through back roads and through a tropical forest in the mountains near Tamarindo where you can spot monkeys, iguanas and other wildlife. The tours are 2-3 hours long and the cost is around $70 USD per person. If you have a child on the back, it's an extra $20 USD. You need to be at least age 16 and have a valid driver's license to go.

Liberia - Ponderosa Adventure Park

- The drive from Tamarindo to Liberia is about an hour and half. Your flight the next day will likely be extremely early so it's nice to check into a hotel near the airport the day prior. and relax at the hotel pool. If you get to Liberia early enough we suggest you visit the **Ponderosa Adventure Park.**

- Ponderosa Adventure Park is an African Safari adventure park located in El Salto, 15km (9 mi) south of Liberia. You take the #1 highway for approximately 15 minutes and you will see signs on the road to turn right where you take a windy road for a few minutes to the park.

- The park has over 70 hectares and has many activities including a safari tour, ziplining and kayaking.

- The safari tour is definitely the most unique experience at the park. You take a tour on a large covered military type transport vehicle through the grounds. There are over 10 different types of African animals and some of them come up to the vehicle to be fed including Giraffes, Zebras and Emu. The animals seem to have plenty of room to roam.

- The cost is $37 USD per person. The website is: **https://ponderosacostarica.com/#**

isclaimer

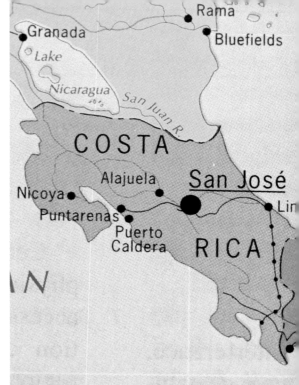

e information provided in this
erary is based on our
periences and research. All
sts and activities are up to
te as per the publication date
this itinerary and subject to
ange. Always do your own
search, check government
bsites for latest travel
ormation and choose
tivities based on your
erests, comfort level and
ility.

Published August, 2022

Visit our YouTube channel!
@AdventureCampitelli

We've created many videos about Costa Rica including the places covered in this itinerary plus videos on things you need to know before you go, and a few videos on what not to do in Costa Rica. Below are links to a few of these videos:

Arenal Travel Guide:
- *https://youtu.be/U6jmvSMCIKs*

Monteverde:
- *https://youtu.be/uKPi89iIY2A*

Tamarindo Travel Guide:
- *https://youtu.be/t39xF36-DYY*

> **Don't dream about it** *Do* **it!**